Fall from Grace

Essential Literary Themes

by Maryellen Lo Bosco

Essential Library

An Imprint of Abdo Publishing | abdopublishing.com

abdopublishing.com

Published by Abdo Publishing, a division of ABDO, PO Box 398166, Minneapolis, Minnesota 55439. Copyright © 2016 by Abdo Consulting Group, Inc. International copyrights reserved in all countries. No part of this book may be reproduced in any form without written permission from the publisher. Essential Library™ is a trademark and logo of Abdo Publishing.

Printed in the United States of America, North Mankato, Minnesota
052015
092015

Cover Photo: Shutterstock Images
Interior Photos: Shutterstock Images, 1; Everett Collection, 13, 26, 55, 65, 71, 83, 89; Bettmann/Corbis, 15; Barry Wetcher/Twentieth Century Fox Film Corporation/Photofest, 16; 20th Century Fox Film Corp./Everett, 18, 21, 23, 29; Columbia Pictures/Photofest, 35, 43; Moviestore/Rex Features/AP Images, 38; NBC/Everett, 41; Mary Evans/Columbia Pictures/Ronald Grant/Everett Collection, 45, 93; CSU Archives/Everett Collection, 49; TriStar Pictures/Everett Collection, 57, 63; Universal Pictures/Photofest, 61; John Jay/Warner Bros. Pictures/Photofest, 69; Frank May/DPA/AP Images, 77; Corbis, 81; Superstock/Everett Collection, 84; Mary Evans Picture Library/Everett Collection, 87; Mary Evans/Ronald Grant/Everett Collection, 91; Photofest, 96

Editor: Mari Kesselring
Series Designer: Maggie Villaume

Library of Congress Control Number: 2015931191
Cataloging-in-Publication Data

Lo Bosco, Maryellen.
 Fall from grace / Maryellen Lo Bosco.
   p. cm. -- (Essential literary themes)
Includes bibliographical references and index.
ISBN 978-1-62403-804-4
1. American literature--Themes, motives--Juvenile literature. 2. American literature--History and criticism--Juvenile literature.   I. Title.
810--dc23

                                                              2015931191

Contents

1

Themes in Literature

*D*o you find yourself drawn to the same types of stories? Are your favorite characters on a quest? Are they seeking revenge? Or are your favorite stories about love? Love, revenge, a quest—these are all examples of themes. Although each story is different, many stories focus on similar themes. You can expand your understanding of the books you read by recognizing the common themes within them.

What Is a Theme?

A theme is a concept or idea that shows up again and again in various works of art, literature, music, theater, film, and other endeavors throughout history. Some themes revolve around a story's plot. For example, a play about a young girl moving away from home and learning the ways of the world would be considered a coming of age story. But themes are not always so easily noticed. For example, a work might have allusions. Allusions are references, sometimes indirect, to other works or historical events. Themes might also relate to specific characters or subjects of a work. For example, many stories present heroes or villains. These common character types are often called archetypes.

How Do You Uncover a Theme?

Themes are presented in different ways in different works, so you may not always be aware of them. Many works have multiple themes. Uncover themes by asking yourself questions about the work. What is the main point or lesson of the story? What is the main conflict? What do the characters want? Where does the story take place? In many cases, themes may not be apparent until after a close study, or analysis, of the text.

What Is an Analysis?

Writing an analysis allows you to explore the themes in a work. In an analysis, you can consider themes in multiple ways. You can describe what themes are present in a work. You can compare one work to another to see how the presentation of a theme differs between the two forms. You can see how the use of a particular theme either supports or rejects society's norms. Rather than attempt to discover the author's purpose in creating a work, an analysis reveals what *you* see in the work.

Raising your awareness of themes through analysis allows you to dive deeper into the work itself. You may begin to see similarities between all creative works that you encounter. You may also improve your own writing by expanding your understanding of how stories use themes to engage readers.

Forming a Thesis

Form your questions about how a theme is presented in a work or multiple works and find answers within the work itself. Then you can create a thesis. The thesis is the key point in your analysis. It is your argument about the work. For example, if you want to argue that the theme of a book is love, your thesis could be worded as follows: Allison Becket's novel *On the Heartless Road* asserts that receiving love is critical to the human experience.

How to Make a Thesis Statement

In an analysis, a thesis statement typically appears at the end of the introductory paragraph. It is usually only one sentence long and states the author's main idea.

Providing Evidence

Once you have formed a thesis, you must provide evidence to support it. Evidence will usually take the form of examples and quotations from the work itself, often including dialogue from a character. You may wish to address what others have written about the work. Quotes from these individuals may help support your claim. If you find any quotes or examples that contradict your thesis, you will need to create an argument against them. For instance: Many critics claim the theme of love is secondary to that of revenge, as the main character, Carly, sabotages the lives of her loved ones throughout the novel. However, the novel's resolution proves that Carly's experience with love is the key to her humanity.

Concluding the Essay

After you have written several arguments and included evidence to support them, finish the essay with

How to Support a Thesis Statement

An analysis should include several arguments that support the thesis's claim. An argument is one or two sentences long and is supported by evidence from the work being discussed. Organize the arguments into paragraphs. These paragraphs make up the body of the analysis.

a conclusion. The conclusion restates the ideas from the thesis and summarizes some of the main points from the essay. The conclusion's final thought often considers additional implications for the essay or gives the reader something to ponder further.

In This Book

In this book, you will read summaries of works, each followed by an analysis. Critical thinking sections will give you a chance to consider other theses and questions about the work. Did you agree with the author's analysis? What other questions are raised by the thesis and its arguments? You can also see other directions the author could have pursued to analyze the work. Then, in the Analyze It section in the final pages of this book, you will have an opportunity to create your own analysis paper.

The Theme of a Fall from Grace

The book you are reading focuses on the theme of a fall from grace. This theme is one of the oldest archetypes in human storytelling. A fall from grace is a moment in a story when a character makes a huge mistake that puts the character at odds with the moral values of his or her society. The character has "fallen" from public opinion and often entered into a realm of evil.

Along with a fall from grace comes the theme of redemption. Characters who fall from grace have the possibility of being redeemed. If a character is redeemed, he has either corrected or made up for the wrongs he committed. The character is reformed. Many fall from grace stories focus on the character's effort to be redeemed. But in others, the character continues his or her fall throughout the story and is never redeemed.

Look for the Guides

Throughout the chapters that analyze the works, thesis statements have been highlighted. The box next to the thesis helps explain what questions are being raised about the work. Supporting arguments have also been highlighted. The boxes next to the arguments help explain how these points support the thesis. The conclusions are also accompanied by explanatory boxes. Look for these guides throughout each analysis.

2

AN OVERVIEW OF

The Crucible

The Crucible, a play in four acts set in the colonial period in the 1600s, portrays an infamous episode in American history—the Salem witch trials. The Salem, Massachusetts, government was a theocracy, as were other early American communities settled by Puritans from England. There was no separation of church and state in Salem. The government was based on religious principles. The Puritans believed witches existed and did the work of the devil. In Salem in 1692, a group of young Puritan girls claimed to have communicated with the devil at the urging of certain adults in the community. Soon a full-blown witch hunt was in progress. Playwright Arthur Miller based his work on some of these events.

The Crucible, based on the Salem witch trails, follows the story of fictional John Proctor.

The Crucible was written in 1952 during another infamous interlude in American history, called the Red Scare, a time when Americans were suspicious of anyone who might be connected to the Communist Party. Many people, including writers and entertainers, were called before Congress by the House Un-American Activities Committee (HUAC). Some politicians believed communism posed a danger to the American way of life. HUAC questioned people, including writers and entertainers, to see if they had communist ties. It was often enough to simply name someone as a communist sympathizer to get them into trouble. Miller wrote *The Crucible* as a commentary on what he saw as a witch hunt for communists.

Unnatural Things

The first act of the play takes place in an upstairs bedroom in the home of Reverend Samuel Parris, who ministers to the congregation of Salem. Reverend Parris is praying beside the bed of his ten-year-old daughter, Betty. She is lying in what appears to be a comatose state. Parris, a widower, is raising Betty with the help of Tituba, a black slave and housekeeper. Also living in the house is Abigail (Abby) Williams, his 17-year-old

Actor Adolphe Menjou takes the oath as he testifies for HUAC in 1947. *The Crucible* criticized the Red Scare.

orphaned niece. Parris has asked the doctor for help, but he sends word that there is nothing he can do for Betty. He says it is time to call in a spiritual expert to look for "unnatural things" as the cause of her illness.[1] In fact, Parris has already called Reverend Hale, an expert on such matters. Another child in the community, Mary Putnam, is also strangely ill.

Right before the children fell ill, Parris found Abby, Betty, and some others in the forest with Tituba. They seemed to have been engaged in a strange ritual. He asks Abby about this activity, as well as why she was fired from her job as a servant to John and Elizabeth Proctor. Abby denies any evildoing or communicating with the devil.

Parris found the girls in the forest with Tituba participating in some type of ritual.

John Proctor has come to Parris's house to find out about the commotion. John and Abby talk privately. He tells her they have no future together, although she doesn't believe it. He had a sexual relationship with Abby while she was living in his house, which is why his wife fired her. John feels tremendous guilt and shame about his relations with Abby. He is trying to repair his damaged marriage. Other people who enter the scene are the Putnams; Rebecca Nurse, a well-respected old woman who has many children and grandchildren; and Giles Corey, one of the Proctors' neighbors. It becomes clear John is also at odds with the church. He dislikes the way Parris preaches.

Reverend Hale, an expert on witchcraft and the devil, finally arrives. Parris tells Hale his niece and daughter were dancing in the forest. Under the pressure of close questioning, Abby accuses Tituba of making her drink chicken blood. Tituba also breaks under interrogation. By the end of the scene, Tituba has admitted to speaking with the devil and seeing others with him. Abby claims to have seen several women with the devil. Betty wakes up and joins in the confession.

Accused

The second act takes place in the house of the Proctors more than a week later. John and Elizabeth are trying to repair their marriage. They also speak of the terrible trouble in town, where more than a dozen people are in jail, having been accused of witchcraft. Mary Warren, the Proctors' servant, is one of the key witnesses. She claims to be one of the victims of the townspeople who have communicated with the devil and now send their spirits out to torment the girls and cause them to fall into trances or fits.

John is angry with Mary and with Elizabeth, who he feels has not forgiven him. Elizabeth believes Abby still has some hold over John. Meanwhile, Hale arrives to question the Proctors about their Christianity. While he is there, representatives from the court come to

Abby admits to John that the girls were only pretending to be possessed.

arrest Elizabeth, who has been called out as a witch, along with several others. John understands Abby is behind his wife's arrest. He vows to go to court to tell the magistrates that Abby told him they never saw any devil and that it was "all sport" for the girls.[2] They were pretending to be possessed. He also demands Mary tell the court the truth.

The Trials

The third act occurs in the meetinghouse, where the trials are taking place. Giles Corey and Francis Nurse have come to the court to attempt to save their wives, who had been named as witches. John has also arrived with Mary. She has promised to tell the truth to the court. The judges hear her testimony. She explains that her fits and fainting spells were not real. But when she is asked to reproduce her false behavior, she cannot do it because she needs the influence of the other girls to put her in the frame of mind for creating a performance. Abby is called in for questioning, but she stands her ground and then falls into a trance. The other girls who are accusers follow her lead. Mary tries to get them to stop, but she cannot.

In desperation, John confesses to the court his adultery with Abby. He hopes this will make them understand that Abby wants to destroy his wife so that she can be with him. The magistrates call Elizabeth in to confirm his story. But Elizabeth denies it to protect him. Thus, the court dismisses John's accusations. Meanwhile, Abby and the girls are now pretending Mary is sending her spirit out to attack them. Mary turns on John and accuses him of witchcraft. He is taken to jail.

Hanging Day

The last act of the play opens on hanging day. Several people are scheduled to hang, including Rebecca Nurse and John Proctor. Elizabeth has been spared for a time because she is pregnant with John's child. Meanwhile, Hale is experiencing a lot of remorse for his part in the proceedings. He has returned to the jail to convince Rebecca and John to confess to witchcraft so that they can save their lives. A confession will earn them punishment but spare them the gallows. Hale entreats Elizabeth to speak to her husband for the same purpose.

John and Elizabeth are granted a moment alone. Elizabeth tells him she has forgiven him for his adultery, but he must forgive himself. She also takes some

In the courtroom, Abby pretends to be in a trance, and the other girls follow her lead.

responsibility for his turning to Abby, saying she was "a cold wife," and asks him for forgiveness.[3] In his desire to be rejoined with his wife again, now that he knows their marriage is redeemed, John tells Elizabeth he plans to confess. But when officials bring him papers to sign, he begins backing away from his confession. He signs the document but then rips it up, unable to go through with blackening his name. When Hale tries to convince Elizabeth to change her husband's mind, she refuses, believing John's stand is the right one. John is taken to the gallows.

3

Moral Compass in *The Crucible*

$\mathcal{S}$ tories of a fall from grace and redemption are found in every culture, perhaps because they express a basic and universal human experience. In order to have a fall from grace, the morality of a society must be clearly defined. In other words, a society must have a clear sense of what is right and what is wrong. People in the society internalize this moral compass. If a person falls away from the "good side," they must find a way to right their moral compass, or achieve redemption, to be accepted into society again. However, individuals also have their own sense of right and wrong, which might differ from societal values. When societal morality

John must gain redemption by following his own moral compass.

differs from a character's idea of right and wrong in a story, it shows that what is "good" can be subjective.

In *The Crucible*, protagonist John Proctor initially falls from grace by betraying his wife. But when he tries to restore his goodness, he is unjustly accused of a worse crime—witchcraft. The play presents an unjust social structure to demonstrate that an individual who wants redemption must navigate by his own moral compass rather than by community values. John achieves redemption after his fall from grace by going against his society's idea of morality and listening instead to his own moral compass.

From the outset of the play, John Proctor is at odds with his community in their interpretations of religious duty and moral norms. He is characterized as a Puritan and a Christian, but not as a man who simply does what the minister says. For example, John has stopped going to church because he doesn't like the way the new minister preaches. When Mr. Putnam criticizes him for not coming to Sabbath meetings on a regular basis, he says, "I have trouble enough without I come five mile to hear him preach only hellfire and bloody damnation. Take it to heart, Mr. Parris. There are many others who stay away from church these days because you hardly ever mention God any more."[1] John is sick of hearing about Hell. He also thinks Parris is materialistic and greedy. He objects to the fact that Parris wants to own the house he lives in and has asked for the deed. When Parris worries that there is a following or "faction" against the church, John defiantly jokes that he means to go out and join this faction.[2]

The town of Salem's response to the witchcraft accusations, when compared to John's reaction, shows the society is acting in an unjust manner. John is portrayed as skeptical about the existence of witches, and he tries to be a voice of reason amid

Argument Two

The second argument looks at the actions of the people of Salem. The argument is: "The town of Salem's response to the witchcraft accusations, when compared to John's reaction, shows the society is acting in an unjust manner."

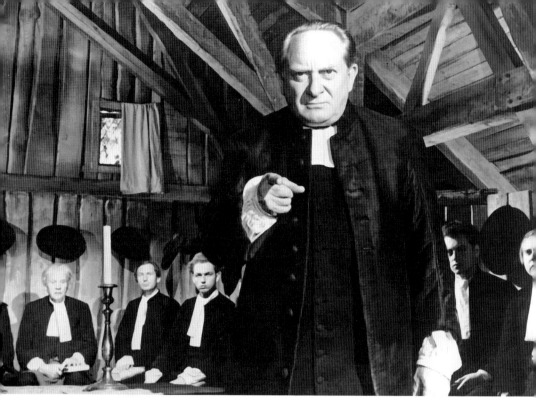

John's attempt to be the voice of reason in his community does not save him from being labeled a witch.

the hysteria in the town. When witchcraft expert Reverend Hale arrives to deal with the issue of witches in Salem, John cautions Hale. He says, "I heard you to be a sensible man, Mr. Hale. I hope you leave some of it in Salem."[3] John recognizes that his society has been acting irresponsibly. But Hale does not take his advice. Instead, Hale presses Abby about what happened in the woods until she accuses several people of trafficking with the devil. Soon the accusations spin out of control, and all the girls who were in the woods begin telling the same story. John's effort to be the voice of reason does nothing to calm his community.

In his effort to save his wife, John confesses to adultery, revealing the source of Abby's ill will against his wife and attempting to gain redemption from his community. His confession occurs after he goes to court with Mary Warren, one of the girls claiming to be possessed. Mary has agreed to tell the court the girls were faking their hysterics and lying when they said people were sending their spirits out to torment them. When this fails to convince the magistrates, John publicly confesses his lechery with Abby so the court will understand she intends to have his wife hanged so she can be with him. He says to the court, "I beg you, sir, I beg you—see her [for] what she is. . . . She thinks to dance with me on my wife's grave! And well she might, for I thought of her softly. God help me, I lusted, and there is a promise in such sweat."[4] In this confession, John reveals his sin for all to see. He attempts to right his moral compass by saving his wife and finding redemption from his community. But since

Argument Three

Next, the author turns to John's forced attempt to gain redemption in his community. The third argument is: "In his effort to save his wife, John confesses to adultery, revealing the source of Abby's ill will against his wife and attempting to gain redemption from his community."

the society has a corrupt moral compass, it doesn't work. The magistrates question his wife separately, and she will not confirm his story. Meanwhile, Mary Warren caves in and accuses John of witchcraft, and he too is jailed.

Argument Four

The final argument examines how John's own moral compass clashes with his society's viewpoints. The argument is: "John has one last chance to receive redemption from his community, but by following his own moral compass, John achieves redemption through his own values instead."

John has one last chance to receive redemption from his community, but by following his own moral compass, John achieves redemption through his own values instead. In act 4, John is told that if he confesses to witchcraft, he will be punished but not hanged. But John knows he is not guilty of witchcraft and doesn't want to admit to something he did not do. During a conversation with Elizabeth, John asks her again for forgiveness for his adultery. She responds that he must forgive himself. She also asks for his forgiveness and says that she was "a cold wife" to him.[5] At this point, John wants to live because he knows his wife has forgiven him and he can finally forgive himself. To appease the community and win his

Although John dies on the gallows at the end of the play, he has been redeemed.

life back, John signs a document admitting his guilt, but then he rips it up. He refuses to admit to witchcraft and lose his good name. In relief, he realizes he is finally redeemed after his fall from grace and tells Hale, "I do think I see some shred of goodness in John Proctor."[6] John recognizes the immorality of his own society as they got caught up in the drama of the witchcraft accusations. Hale urges Elizabeth to "Go to him, take his shame away!" because he thinks John is ashamed to lie to save his life.[7] But she replies, "He have his goodness now. God forbid I take it from him!"[8] John has achieved redemption after his fall from grace by going against his society's idea of morality and listening instead to his own moral compass.

John Proctor, characterized as a man who initially shares his community's values, falls from grace by cheating on his wife. But as time goes on, the society's values seem shallow and hypocritical to him. By using his own moral compass, John restores his goodness, first by atoning for the sin against his wife and accepting responsibility for it, then by forgiving himself, and finally by refusing to support a communal lie about the nature of evil. John loses his life by sticking to the truth and following his own moral compass.

Conclusion

The conclusion restates the thesis and summarizes the arguments made in support of the thesis.

Thinking Critically

Now it's your turn to assess the essay. Consider these questions:

1. Which is the strongest argument in the essay? Why?

2. Do you agree that redemption ultimately comes from inside a person rather than from society? Why or why not?

3. Is it possible for a person's moral compass to malfunction? Why or why not?

4. Is it possible for a person to be wrong about what will bring them redemption? Why or why not?

Other Approaches

The previous essay is just one example of how to consider the fall from grace in this play. The theme of a fall from grace in *The Crucible* can be considered in multiple ways. Another approach might focus on how John's religion guides his moral compass but not the morality of the town of Salem. Yet another approach could consider the historical moment in which the play was written and first performed.

Redemption and Puritan Ethics

The Crucible is set in Salem, Massachusetts, in 1692. At this time, the town was populated by Puritans, European Protestants who had strict ideas about religion and the difference between good and evil. The historical background of the play's setting could be a launching pad for an essay that looks at how the play reflects Puritan values. A thesis statement for an analysis that uses this approach could be: Although John Proctor dies because he confessed his sin and thus exposed himself to charges of witchcraft, he has still attained redemption by following the ethical principles of his religion.

The Crucible and Historical Context

Considering the historical moment in which *The Crucible* was first written and produced brings additional depth to the play and John's fall from grace. Miller wrote the play during the Red Scare, paralleling it to the modern-day witch hunt he saw around him. A thesis statement for an analysis that uses this approach could be: People saved themselves by accusing others, both in *The Crucible* and during the Red Scare, but fell from grace and could not redeem themselves.

4

AN OVERVIEW OF

Crime and Punishment

*C*rime and Punishment was published in 1866 by the Russian novelist Fyodor Dostoevsky. Dostoevsky wrote about the complex motivations of human beings with great depth and understanding. This novel, the first of his masterpieces, tackles the themes of suffering, love, and redemption.

The Murder

Rodion Raskolnikov (Rodya), a poor university student, has recently dropped out of school because he can no longer pay his tuition or the rent for his cramped room in Saint Petersburg, Russia. When the novel opens, he is on his way to see the pawnbroker, Alyona Ivanovna.

Crime and Punishment focuses on the story of Rodion Raskolnikov, a poor young student.

She is an old, ugly woman who lives with her stepsister, Lizaveta. The community believes she cheats her clients and mistreats Lizaveta. Rodya leaves Alyona his pledge and says he will return with a valuable silver cigarette case in a few days' time.

After visiting Alyona, he drops in on a seedy tavern for a drink and meets Semyon Marmeladov, a raging alcoholic who feels compelled to tell Rodya his story. Marmeladov has repeatedly lost his job as a civil servant because of his drunkenness. His eldest daughter, Sonya, has been persuaded by her stepmother, Katerina, to work as a prostitute to support the starving family. Rodya walks home with Marmeladov and leaves the family the remaining money in his pocket.

When Rodya gets home, the cleaning lady hands him a letter from his mother. In this letter, which contains money, he finds out that his sister Dunya has left her position as a governess in disgrace after the woman of the house accused her of trying to seduce her husband. In reality, the husband, Arkady Svidrigailov, had been sexually harassing Dunya. But Dunya's name was cleared after Svidrigailov confessed his behavior. Now Dunya has accepted a marriage proposal from Pyotr Luzhin, a haughty civil servant. Dunya and Rodya's mother are on their way to town for the wedding. In the letter, Rodya's mother explains that Luzhin can help Rodya's career. Rodya feels rage and frustration after reading the letter because he knows his mother and sister are sacrificing his sister's happiness for his benefit.

Rodya decides to go through with a plan he has been brooding on, which is to kill Alyona the pawnbroker and steal from her. Rodya takes an ax from his kitchen and prepares a counterfeit pledge—a piece of wood he has wrapped up and bound with thread—to take along with him. When Alyona turns her back to unwrap the pledge, he hits her over the head with the blunt end of the ax a few times and kills her. While he is in the other room, Lizaveta comes in. Before she can do anything, Rodya swings the ax and hits her on the head with the blade side, killing her too. He gets home and falls into a feverish sleep.

Fallout

Rodya regains consciousness after a few days and learns his landlady has called in the doctor, Zossimov. Rodya's school friend, Dmitri Razumikhin, has also stopped by to check on Rodya. Meanwhile Luzhin arrives, but Rodya goes out of his way to insult him. Rodya then goes

Rodya decides to kill Alyona, steal her money, and restart his life.

out and happens upon an accident in which a drunken Marmeladov has been run over by a carriage driver. He takes the dying Marmeladov home. He meets Sonya, the eldest daughter, for the first time. When he returns home, his sister and mother are waiting for him.

Suspicion

When Rodya sees his sister, whom he hasn't seen in a few years, he tells her he will disown her if she marries Luzhin. Dunya insists she is marrying for her own benefit and that Luzhin will be an honorable husband. The three of them plan to meet with Luzhin to iron out their differences, since Luzhin has been offended by Rodya's treatment. At the end of this conversation, Sonya arrives to invite Rodya to her father's funeral dinner.

Later Rodya decides he wants to visit the detective Porfiry Petrovich, who is leading the murder investigation. He feels compelled to see if Petrovich suspects him as the murderer. When he meets Petrovich, he immediately knows the detective is on to him.

Svidrigailov suddenly shows up at Rodya's place. Svidrigailov's wife has died and left money to Dunya. Svidrigailov also wants to give her some money for the trouble he caused her. After this discussion, Rodya leaves to meet his family and Luzhin. Dunya is hoping to resolve the quarrel between her brother and fiancé, but Luzhin simply adds fuel to the fire by insinuating that Dunya is glad Svidrigailov has come to Saint Petersburg in pursuit of her. Dunya becomes furious and breaks off the engagement. Everyone is pleased about her decision, especially Rodya's friend Razumikhin, who is in love with Dunya and now sees a clear path for his own courtship. Rodya, knowing his friend will take care of his family, tells his mother and sister he needs to separate from them for a while.

Rodya visits Sonya as promised. He begins the visit by torturing her with the idea that if something happens to her, Katerina and the children will end up homeless. She cries out to him that God will never allow that to happen. Rodya laughs and says that maybe there is no God. Then he bows down to Sonya, saying he is bowing to all of suffering humanity. He finds out Sonya was friends with Lizaveta and that they would read the Bible together. He demands that she read to him the story of how Jesus raised Lazarus from the dead. He departs, saying he will return again to tell her who killed Lizaveta.

The Confession

At the funeral dinner, Katerina gets into an argument with her landlady, which results in the family being evicted from the building. Rodya leaves to visit Sonya. He tells her about the eviction and also confesses to the murders. Sonya embraces him, promising not to abandon him. She assumes Rodya committed the crime because he was hungry and desperate for money. He sets

Rodya meets with Sonya. He promises to tell her who killed her friend Lizaveta.

her straight, however, explaining he believed he had the right to put himself above the law. He did not want to submit to the grinding life that had been allotted to him by fate.

Sonya asks him to repent what he has done before God and to turn himself in to the authorities. At the end of this conversation, a neighbor comes in to tell Sonya that Katerina has gone mad. Katerina dies. Svidrigailov appears to tell Rodya that he used some of the money he'd planned to give to Dunya for Katerina's funeral expenses and to take care of the children, who must now go to an orphanage. He also tells Rodya he knows about the murders. He says has been eavesdropping from a room in the same apartment where Sonya also rents a room.

The Suicide

Petrovich visits Rodya in an attempt to get him to confess to the murders. After he leaves, Rodya looks for Svidrigailov and threatens to kill him if he tries to use the information about the murders as a weapon against Dunya. Svidrigailov claims he is over Dunya. But, in fact, he has written Dunya a letter alluding to her brother's crime. He uses it to lure her to his room. He then tells her Rodya is a murderer, but he will help the family if she agrees to marry him. When she refuses, he threatens to rape her but then lets her go. Afterward, he visits Sonya and gives her money and receipts for money for her siblings, whom he has provided for. The next day, he commits suicide by shooting himself.

When Rodya sees his family again, he tells Dunya he has no remorse for the murders. Nonetheless, he goes to Sonya to pick up a cross she promised to give him. He puts it around his neck before he enters the police station and finally confesses his crime.

Epilogue

Rodya is given eight years of hard labor in Siberia, and Sonya follows him. He gets a light sentence because he confessed without being forced to do so, and his friends

Eventually, Rodya must serve out his punishment for the crime he committed.

also testify on his behalf. Meanwhile, Razumikhin and Dunya marry, and Rodya's mother dies, broken by the knowledge of her son's fate. Rodya is still not sorry for what he did and even regrets not killing himself. He feels isolated from his fellow prisoners, although Sonya has become something of a mother to all of them.

Sonya visits Rodya regularly, and one day when he meets her outside, he breaks down and cries and embraces her. He realizes he loves her. Although he still has seven years on his prison term, he experiences an infinite love for Sonya that night and begins reading the New Testament. He feels united with her, and it seems he is finally on the road to redemption.

5

Biblical Fall in *Crime and Punishment*

The Bible holds some of the early known representations of a fall from grace in the story of the first man and woman—Adam and Eve—in Genesis. In this story, a serpent tempts Eve to eat fruit from a tree in the Garden of Eden that God has forbidden them from touching. Eve eats the fruit and gives some to Adam too. As a result, God banishes Adam and Eve from the Garden of Eden forever. In the Bible, this is explained as the story of how sin originated, and it is commonly referred to as the Fall. Many works that deal with a fall from grace allude to this story. Christlike figures

The story of Rodya's crime and resulting punishment alludes to stories in the Bible.

may also appear in a fall from grace moment to grant forgiveness to the sinner.

In *Crime and Punishment*, the characters show a range of emotions, from the sublime to the ridiculous. Although the cast of characters contains a world of emotions, the plot that puts them into motion is fairly simple: a young man, Rodya, kills a pawnbroker and her sister, thereby casting himself out of the community.

When Rodya meets Sonya it seems that she may hold the key to his forgiveness. *Crime and Punishment* alludes to biblical ideas about sin and forgiveness in Rodya's fall from grace and his eventual redemption through the Christlike love of Sonya.

Rodya's fall from grace begins when he broods over his poverty and is tempted to commit a heinous crime. Rodya is a brilliant but angry intellectual who must depend on handouts from his mother and sister to pay his university expenses. He lives in one tiny room and wears the same clothes every day. One day Rodya stops at a café for tea and overhears two young men talking about how Alyona, the pawnbroker, cheats people and uses her half sister, Lizaveta, like a slave. One of the young men remarks that he could kill and rob Alyona without remorse. He says someone could steal her money and distribute it to people who could use it for good purposes. "What does the death of this stupid, consumptive, and wicked old crone mean in the balance? No more than the life of a louse or a cockroach, and not even that much, because the old crone is harmful," the young man says.[1] In a biblical sense, this conversation is similar to Eve being tempted by the serpent in the Garden of Eden. Rodya starts thinking about what the young man said. He's tempted by the idea of having Alyona's money.

Rodya decides to kill Alyona and take some of her wealth to restart his life.

Sonya is set up early in the novel as a Christ figure who is the key to her father's redemption. **In a seedy**

Argument Two

In the second argument, the author turns to discussing Sonya as a Christ figure in the novel. The argument is: "Sonya is set up early in the novel as a Christ figure who is the key to her father's redemption."

tavern, Rodya meets Marmeladov, Sonya's father, who recounts losing his job. Marmeladov's family suffers extreme poverty, so his wife has asked his daughter from a previous marriage to become a prostitute to earn money. Sonya agrees to sacrifice herself for the family. According to Christian theology, Jesus has to atone for the sins of man by entering the world and suffering death by crucifixion. Similarly, Sonya atones for her father's inadequacies. Marmeladov says in his drunken rant, "[Jesus] will come and ask, 'Where is the daughter who gave herself . . . for a stranger's little children? Where is the daughter who pitied her earthly father? . . . And He will say 'Come! I have already forgiven you once. . . . And now, too, your many sins are forgiven.'"[2] Similar to Jesus, Marmeladov believes Sonya will be rewarded for atoning for her father's sins, despite committing a sin by engaging in prostitution.

Argument Three

As a Christ figure, Sonya becomes Rodya's friend, confessor, and redeemer. After Rodya commits his crime, he has an urge to confess his sin and eventually

In the final argument, the author considers how Sonya's forgiveness of Rodya redeems him. The final argument is: "As a Christ figure, Sonya becomes Rodya's friend, confessor, and redeemer."

Marmeladov, *right*, confides in Rodya that despite his daughter's profession, her sins will be forgiven.

confides in Sonya. The day before he confesses to her, he asks her to read from the Bible the story of Lazarus's resurrection. In this story, a woman asks Jesus to raise her brother from the dead. Before Jesus performs the miracle, he says, "'I am the resurrection, and the life: he that believeth in me, though he were dead, yet shall he live.'"[3] Rodya is not a Christian, but he understands Sonya will be his salvation. Sonya convinces him to confess. She says, "Go now, this minute, stand in the crossroads, bow down, and first kiss the earth you have defiled . . . and say aloud to everyone: 'I have killed!' Then God will send you life again."[4] Rodya follows her advice and experiences relief and happiness when he bows down. However, he hardens when he gets to Siberia and feels completely cut off from humanity. But one day, when he and Sonya find themselves alone for a moment, he realizes he loves her. He "flung himself down at her feet" and "there was no longer any doubt that he loved her, loved her infinitely . . . they were resurrected by love; the heart of each held infinite sources of life for the heart of the other."[5] Sonya is Rodya's key to redemption.

It is only through Sonya's Christlike love that Rodya is able to finally experience redemption. Dostoevsky uses the Christian idea of the Fall and redemption to show how a man can save himself by opening himself up to divine love. This love may be channeled through another human being—which, in the case of this novel, is the Christlike Sonya.

Conclusion

In the conclusion, the author restates the thesis and summarizes the arguments made in support of the thesis. The author reiterates that it is Sonya's Christlike love that is the key to Rodya's redemption.

Thinking Critically

Now it's your turn to assess the essay. Consider these questions:

1. Do you agree with the author's thesis that Rodya has been redeemed at the end of the story? Why or why not?

2. The author talks about Sonya as a Christlike figure. What other evidence could be used to argue she is a Christ figure in the novel?

3. Is Rodya the only character who needs redemption? Do other characters seem to fall from grace?

Other Approaches

The theme of a fall from grace in *Crime and Punishment* can be considered in multiple ways. Another approach might be to consider how nihilism, or the idea that life has no meaning, presents itself in the novel and conflicts with the idea of a fall from grace and the need for redemption. The second approach looks at how suffering is showcased as a requirement for achieving redemption.

The Nihilistic Twin

Svidrigailov represents nihilism, the idea that life has no ultimate meaning. Like Rodya, Svidrigailov has vices. He sexually harasses Dunya and uses her brother's crime to try to take advantage of her. An essay that considers Svidrigailov's lack of redemption could examine how it compares to Rodya's story. A thesis for this approach could be: Svidrigailov is Rodya's dark twin, and his nihilistic approach to life—in which one fulfills every sensual desire, even at the expense of others—cannot result in redemption.

Suffering as Purification

Another approach might emphasize the role of suffering in the novel, which is common in the Christian idea of redemption. Rodya is plagued by guilt after he commits the murders. And, once he confesses, he must serve years of hard labor as punishment for his crime. A thesis for this approach could be: Rodya can be made spiritually whole and redeemed only after he suffers sufficiently for his sins and becomes purified enough to receive the grace of redemption.

6

AN OVERVIEW OF
Frankenstein

*P*ublished in 1818, Mary Shelley's *Frankenstein* is a tale within a tale. Robert Walton, an intrepid voyager to the North Pole, tells the reader the tale. The 28-year-old explorer hopes to makes a scientific discovery or, at the very least, see some part of the Arctic that has never been visited by man. Walton is writing to his sister, first before he sets off and later from his sea vessel. Passing merchant ships carry his letters back to England.

In one letter, Walton tells his sister how his ship was hemmed in by ice for a time. As they wait for the ice to melt, the crew members see two strange sights. First, through their telescope, they see an enormous man driving a sledge pulled by dogs across the ice plains. Then they see a man in a second sledge, pulled by one dog, floating on a large piece of ice. Walton's

Frankenstein is a popular tale that has been told in many different formats since the original book was published.

crew rescues the man, who is well educated and speaks English. Walton easily makes friends with the intelligent and overwrought stranger—Victor Frankenstein. Frankenstein finds out Walton is on a voyage of discovery. He learns that Walton believes "one man's life or death [is] . . . a small price to pay for the acquirement of the knowledge."[1] Frankenstein then feels compelled to tell Walton his story.

Frankenstein's Story

Frankenstein is born into a family of wealth and privilege in Geneva, Switzerland. His tender and loving parents raise him along with an adopted sister, Elizabeth, the orphaned child of an Italian nobleman. The two grow up as siblings, although their mother expects they will marry when they come of age. Frankenstein's parents have two more boys as well, William and Ernest. Frankenstein's idyllic childhood is also graced by Henry Clerval, his best friend.

From early childhood, Frankenstein has an interest in science. Frankenstein enrolls at a university to study natural philosophy and chemistry and does very well. But what grabs his intense interest is the origin of the life force. After much labored study, he discovers the

The Creature lies on a metal gurney in Frankenstein's laboratory. Once he brings the Creature to life, Frankenstein is terrified by it.

cause of life and learns how to give life to lifeless matter. Soon he rushes headlong into the creation of a living being. He must work in secret and haunt dissecting rooms, slaughterhouses, and graveyards to get the body parts and organs he needs. However, when he brings his Creature to life, he is horrified and disgusted. He runs out of his laboratory.

Henry, Frankenstein's childhood friend, has also come to study at the university. He runs into Frankenstein the morning after he has abandoned the Creature. The two men return to Frankenstein's rooms. Frankenstein then collapses. The months of feverish labor catch up to him all at once. He's confined to bed for several months. While Henry nurses him back to health, in his feverish state Frankenstein raves about the Creature. But he never actually tells Henry what he has done.

In the spring, Frankenstein's father writes to tell him his brother William has been strangled to death. On his way back home in a fierce rainstorm, Frankenstein sees the Creature and suddenly realizes he is the murderer. When Frankenstein gets home, he learns a beloved family servant, Justine, is accused of the murder, because she had a picture that belonged to William in her pocket. Frankenstein knows somehow the Creature has framed her. Frankenstein tries to save Justine, but he will not share his terrible secret with anyone. Justine goes to the gallows.

Frankenstein attempts to cope with his guilty burden by spending some time in nature. While he is mountain climbing, the Creature catches up with him. Frankenstein accuses him of murder and berates him. The Creature says Frankenstein has a duty toward him and must comply with a request. If he does not, the Creature threatens he will "glut the maw of death, until it be satiated with the blood of your remaining friends."[2] He also asks Frankenstein to listen to his story so he can understand why he has turned so evil. Frankenstein agrees.

The Creature's Story

The Creature tells Frankenstein about how he awoke to consciousness, innocent as a baby. He finds his way into the forest and begins foraging for food. He soon learns that all humans run away from him because of his hideous appearance. However, he comes upon a house in the woods and begins secretly spying on the family there.

At one point the young man of the house, Felix, is teaching his Arabian fiancé, Safie, the English language. In this way, the Creature learns English. He also comes across some books that help him. He finally gets up the courage to befriend the blind old man who lives in the cottage with his two children and his son's fiancé. Unfortunately, the young people find him with their father and beat him away. The Creature realizes he can never be accepted into human society. Soon after, he runs into Frankenstein's little brother, who also rejects him. The Creature kills the boy and frames the servant to get revenge on Frankenstein. Since his creator brought him so much misery, the Creature now demands a mate and companion for himself so he does not have to be alone.

Although he is disgusted and horrified by the idea of creating another creature, Frankenstein decides to grant the Creature's wish. After some time passes, he begins his grisly labors. But shortly before he is finished, he realizes he cannot go through with it. What if the two of them combine forces to wreak havoc on mankind? He worries they will give birth to "a race of devils."[3] With these thoughts in his mind, Frankenstein destroys his second creation. The Creature, who has been watching him, bursts in and swears vengeance, vowing to be with Frankenstein on his wedding night.

The Creature's Revenge

Soon after Frankenstein leaves the remote island in Scotland where he has been working, he finds out his friend Henry, who was also in Scotland, has been murdered. Frankenstein decides to return home and protect his remaining loved ones. He plans to kill the Creature if he gets an opportunity. Frankenstein marries Elizabeth when he comes home. But true to his promise, the Creature kills Frankenstein's new wife in her bridal bed. Soon Frankenstein's father dies of grief over

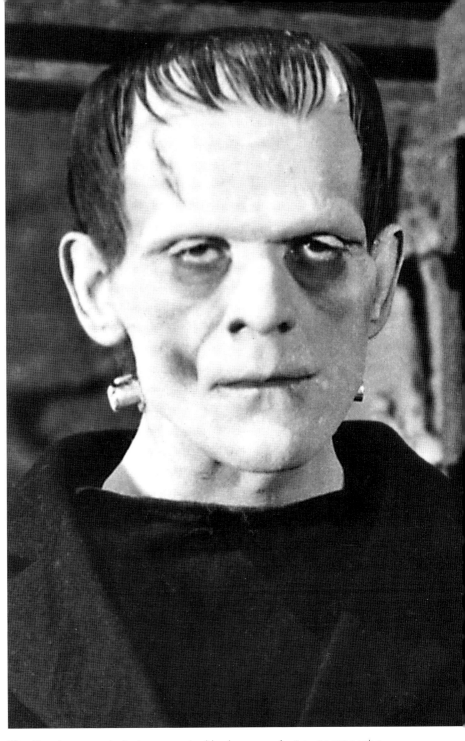

The Creature wants to be accepted by humans, but everyone who sees him is afraid.

Elizabeth's death. At this point, Frankenstein finally goes to a magistrate and confesses his whole story. But the judge doesn't really believe him and thinks he may be crazy. Frankenstein vows to track down the Creature and kill him. Frankenstein chases the Creature all over Europe. The Creature, in turn, taunts Frankenstein by leaving messages in various locations. Eventually the Creature heads north, to the mountains of ice and the frozen sea, which is where both of them run into Walton.

Walton's Final Letters

When Walton picks up his own story again, he tells his sister Frankenstein is near to death and he and his shipmates are stuck in the ice and unable to move. Walton has already lost several crew members. Some of the men have asked him to turn back home if there is a break in the ice, because they will surely die. Frankenstein hears this conversation and exhorts the men to be brave and not give up on obtaining glory. However, once the ice breaks and Walton sees an opening to turn south, he does so. He is very disappointed about giving up his quest but will not lead unwilling men any further into danger.

The Creature mourns the death of Frankenstein, his creator.

Soon after, Frankenstein dies. The Creature finds
him on the ship, and Walton walks in on the Creature
as he mourns over Frankenstein's corpse. The Creature
seems to grieve for the evil he has done. Walton berates
the Creature and calls him a hypocrite, but the Creature
tells him not to worry about him causing any further
destruction. He plans to build his own funeral pyre and
burn himself to death. The Creature then jumps out of
the cabin window and onto an ice raft. Walter watches
the raft moving away from him on the ocean waves.

7

A Cautionary Tale

$\mathcal{M}$any fall from grace stories are told as cautionary tales. They warn the reader of the consequences of heading down an unjust path. They pass on knowledge of how pride, greed, and other vices can result in a fall from grace. In a similar way, characters who fall from grace may serve as warnings to other characters who are at risk for a similar fate.

The story of *Frankenstein*, Mary Shelley's famous novel about the dangers of developing technology without thinking about its moral and ethical consequences, is told as a framed narrative. The largest frame is the story of the intrepid explorer, Robert Walton, who has a lot in common with Victor Frankenstein, whom he rescues on the Arctic Sea. Both

Victor Frankenstein's fall from grace begins when he creates a living creature.

men want to do something unique and make a lasting mark on the world. Both seem willing to do anything to achieve glory. Frankenstein tells Walton his tale, which contains the embedded narrative of the Creature that Frankenstein has brought to life. The framed narrative of *Frankenstein* allows for Frankenstein's fall from grace to become a cautionary tale for Walton, who considers the consequences of his actions and thus narrowly avoids his own fall from grace.

Frankenstein responds to Walton's desire to achieve recognition at any cost by telling him his own story as a lesson. Walton recounts this conversation to his sister, who is the recipient of the four letters at the beginning of the novel. Walton is on the cusp of realizing his lifelong dream

Thesis Statement

The author states her thesis: "The framed narrative of *Frankenstein* allows for Frankenstein's fall from grace to become a cautionary tale for Walton, who considers the consequences of his actions and thus narrowly avoids his own fall from grace."

Argument One

First, the author looks at how Frankenstein recognizes that Walton is headed down a dangerous professional path. The first argument states: "Frankenstein responds to Walton's desire to achieve recognition at any cost by telling him his own story as a lesson."

of exploring the North Pole. Walton and his crew rescue Frankenstein when their ship is temporarily stranded in the ice. When Walton tells Frankenstein of his grand ambition, saying a man's life or death is a small price to pay for acquiring knowledge, Frankenstein draws back in horror. He says, "Unhappy man! Do you share my madness? Have you drunk also of that intoxicating draught? Hear me—let me reveal my tale, and you will dash that cup from your lips!"[1] Frankenstein tells Walton he still has hope and his life before him, unlike Frankenstein, who has already fallen from grace. Frankenstein says that perhaps Walton can take a moral from his story.

Frankenstein does not stop to think about the potential consequences of continuing down his path of discovery. Neither does he hesitate for a minute to give life to the most complex of animals—man. Once he decides to create a manlike creature, he becomes obsessed with

Argument Two

The second argument considers how Frankenstein's story reveals the mistakes he made that led to his fall from grace. The second argument is: "Frankenstein does not stop to think about the potential consequences of continuing down his path of discovery."

the idea, raiding graves and dissecting rooms to obtain the materials he needs. On a dark and stormy night in November, he brings the hideous being to life. He recognizes too late how alien and repulsive the Creature is, even to his own creator. Frankenstein failed to consider the consequences of his plan before acting on it.

Argument Three

The third argument shows how Frankenstein did not work to redeem himself after his fall from grace. The third argument is: "Frankenstein is unable to redeem himself from his fall from grace because he does not take responsibility for his actions."

Frankenstein is unable to redeem himself from his fall from grace because he does not take responsibility for his actions. Frankenstein never tells anyone else about his experiment. Two years pass, and he is called back to Geneva after his brother is murdered. He encounters the Creature on his journey home and intuitively realizes the Creature is the murderer, but he decides not to tell anybody. Even after the faithful servant, Justine, is jailed and sentenced to death for the crime, Frankenstein makes no effort to save her by revealing the truth. He even selfishly says, "The tortures of the accused did not equal mine; she was sustained by innocence, but the

Dangerous and angry, the Creature wreaks havoc on
Frankenstein's loved ones as Frankenstein fails to protect them.

fangs of remorse tore my bosom and would not forgo their hold."[2]

When the Creature finally gets a chance to tell his maker how human beings rejected him and why he now wants Frankenstein to make him a companion, Frankenstein is horrified. But he has no sympathy for the Creature's suffering. Frankenstein ultimately refuses to create a companion for the Creature, who has now sworn to kill everyone Frankenstein loves. Frankenstein still stays silent, however, even after the Creature kills his best friend and his bride. He does not protect his wife, even though the Creature has promised to kill her. Instead, he carries pistols in case "the fiend should openly attack me," giving little thought to the fact that the fiend kills the people Frankenstein loves.[3] Finally, after his father dies of grief, Frankenstein vows to spend the remainder of his life hunting down the fiend he has created. But it is too little, too late.

The framed narrative allows for Frankenstein's tale to lead to Walton's redemption. Walton is

Argument Four

In the fourth argument, the author asserts that by hearing Frankenstein's tale, Walton becomes a changed man. The final argument is: "The framed narrative allows for Frankenstein's tale to lead to Walton's redemption."

Even though the Creature vowed to kill Frankenstein's bride, Frankenstein does not protect her.

headed down a similar road to disaster as Frankenstein, fueled by his own egotism and desire for glory. While his desire to achieve something in the realm of science is noble, his attitude that the price of his glory is worth any sacrifice is not. His ship is surrounded by mountains of ice. If there is a break in the ice, he wants to go forward. However, his men want to turn back. The framed narrative structure of the novel allows Walton to hear and learn from Frankenstein's failures. After hearing Frankenstein's story, Walton changes. He thinks about how the lives of the men he is responsible for are being endangered by his ambition. Walton has taken Frankenstein's story to heart. He decides to turn back when he sees a way to go south. He realizes he has no right to put more lives in danger simply for his own honor and glory.

Due to the framed narrative in *Frankenstein*, Walton is influenced by Frankenstein's tale. Frankenstein's sad story ends with both his and the Creature's deaths, while Walton's story begins with him putting aside his dreams of greatness. He chooses a less grandiose but more honorable path in not forcing his crew into danger.

Thus, Walton manages, through the example set by Frankenstein, to save himself from a terrible fall from grace. Walton redeems himself by putting the humanity of others ahead of his own need for fame and recognition.

Conclusion

In the conclusion, the author restates how the framed narrative in *Frankenstein* allows Walton to avoid a fall from grace. The author summarizes the arguments made in the analysis.

Thinking Critically

Now it's your turn to assess the essay. Consider these questions:

1. Do you agree with the author's thesis about *Frankenstein*? What would you add?

2. Do you sympathize with Frankenstein's dilemma of not wanting to share his terrible secret? Why or why not?

3. Do you agree that Walton is deeply affected by Frankenstein's story? Why or why not?

Other Approaches

This essay is just one possible approach to thinking about how the themes of a fall from grace and redemption can be applied to *Frankenstein.* Here are two additional ways to think about the same themes. One considers a comparison between Frankenstein and the myth of Prometheus. The other considers the novel from a psychological standpoint.

Frankenstein as the Anti-Prometheus

Frankenstein can be compared to the hero Prometheus, who according to the ancient Greek myth stole fire from the gods to make men more like the gods. In fact, Mary Shelley herself calls Frankenstein "the modern-day Prometheus." But Frankenstein unlocks the secret of life to make himself more like God, rather than sharing that power with humanity. A thesis that takes this approach could be: While Prometheus finds redemption and forgiveness through the gods, Frankenstein is not restored to grace because he breaks a sacred boundary simply for his own personal glory.

Frankenstein as a Narcissist

Another way to look at Frankenstein's mad pursuit of science is through a psychological lens. Frankenstein could be viewed as a narcissist, someone who is extremely self-centered and selfish. He is unaware of the Creature's needs and struggles. A thesis that considers Frankenstein as a narcissist could be: As a classic narcissist, Victor Frankenstein never gets beyond his self-interest, and so it is impossible for him to experience true redemption, which requires the ability to humble oneself and see that sometimes someone else's needs are more important than one's own.

8

AN OVERVIEW OF

Things Fall Apart and *Macbeth*

*T*hings Fall Apart, written by Chinua Achebe, a renowned Nigerian author, tells the story of how the Ibo tribe of Nigeria was subdued by the British colonists. Achebe said he wrote the story because he wanted the world to know his people had a long and venerable history before the arrival of European settlers. The story takes place sometime between 1890 and 1915.

William Shakespeare wrote *Macbeth* in 1606. In addition to being a dramatist and actor, Shakespeare was a shrewd businessman. To flatter the new monarch, James I, he set this play in Scotland, where James

Nigerian writer Chinua Achebe wrote *Things Fall Apart.*

originated, and loosely based the play on Scottish history from the 1000s CE. He also included witches because James I was enthusiastic about the subject. *Macbeth* is a story of how a good man turns to the dark side.

Things Fall Apart

Okonkwo is known in all Umuofia, a group of nine villages, for beating Amalinze the Cat in a wrestling match. He bested the champion when he was still a teenager, and over the years he has gained wealth and respect in his tribe. When the story opens, Okonkwo is in his thirties. He is a farmer, battle-tested warrior, and tribal elder. Although well respected, he is also known as a man with a quick and violent temper who doesn't suffer fools gladly. Okonkwo has overcome tremendous odds, which is partly why he is impatient with others. He is the son of a lazy father who never accumulated enough wealth to provide for his children. When it came time for Okonkwo to start his own farm, he had to borrow seed yams from two wealthy men in the village. He lost almost everything in his first harvest due to unusually bad weather. But he eventually managed to succeed through extraordinary hard work and perseverance.

Although a fearless warrior, Okonkwo is afraid of one thing—that he might ever be considered weak and cowardly like his father. His whole life has been, to some degree, an exercise in proving to others—but most of all to himself—that he is not like his father. For this reason, he is sometimes overly harsh in his displays of manliness. This streak of excessiveness is why he takes part in the killing of his foster son. This boy, Ikemefuna, and a young maiden were given to the village by another tribe to make up for the killing of one of Umuofia's women and to prevent a war. The maiden was given to a man who lost his wife. Okonkwo, as a respected elder, was asked to care for the boy. Okonkwo's eldest son, Nwoye, who is gentle and unlike his father, became good friends with Ikemefuna.

One day, the priestess Chielo tells the village elders that the Oracle of the Hills and the Caves, whom she serves, has decreed that Ikemefuna must be taken into the forest and killed. The men of the village undertake this task reluctantly. The oldest man in the tribes tells Okonkwo not to take part because he has become the boy's father. But because Okonkwo fears being thought of as weak, he insists on coming along and then delivers the death blow to Ikemefuna with his machete. Nwoye is devastated.

Okonkwo's Fall

After some time passes, an elder in the tribe dies. The men of the village mourn his passing with a funeral rite that simulates war. Okonkwo shoots off his gun at the funeral, but it malfunctions and explodes, killing one of the young sons of the dead elder. In keeping with tribal custom, Okonkwo must flee the village with his family for seven years because he has offended the earth goddess.

When seven years have passed, Okonkwo returns home and tries to take up where he left off. But while he was gone, white men came to Umuofia and nearby villages. They are interfering with the tribal way of life. He learns the Christian missionaries have won some men of standing to their faith, and the white newcomers have begun imposing their government and laws on his people. To Okonkwo's dismay, Nwoye becomes a Christian. Then, one of the new Christian converts unmasks an ancestral spirit (a man dressed as the spirit) at a tribal feast. At the prompting of Okonkwo, men of the tribe burn down the Christian church in retribution.

A European missionary reads to two Africans. Okonkwo's way of life changes when missionaries arrive.

Three days later, the white district commissioner tricks the tribal elders into coming to a meeting to discuss what happened. He then jails them. The village must pay a large fine to have the men released. Once the men are free, the nine villages of Umuofia assemble for a meeting in the marketplace to decide what to do about the white intruders. When a court messenger and four of his subordinates are sent to stop the meeting, Okonkwo strikes the leader down with his machete. But no one in Umuofia, despite the number of people present, jumps up to catch the others as they run away. Okonkwo then realizes that his people will not fight a war against the white settlers. When the district commissioner later comes to arrest Okonkwo for his crime, he learns Okonkwo has hung himself. Because of his suicide, Okonkwo is denied a proper burial by his people. Like his father before him, he dies in disgrace.

Summary of *Macbeth*

This play famously opens with three witches meeting in a rainstorm, announcing their plan to meet again later with Macbeth. In the next scene, there is news from the battlefield. King Duncan has been putting down a rebellion with the help of loyal thanes, who include Macbeth and Banquo. Macbeth has defeated the traitor, the Thane of Cawdor. After their final battles, Macbeth and Banquo encounter the witches. The witches tell Macbeth he will become Thane of Cawdor and eventually king. Then they tell Banquo his descendants will be kings, but Banquo himself will never be king. Then the witches vanish. Moments later, messengers from King Duncan arrive. They tell Macbeth that he has been named Thane of Cawdor. Surprised that one

When he returns from war, Macbeth hears a prophecy that he will one day become king.

The three witches tell Macbeth and Banquo their prophecies.

of the witches' prophecies was true, Macbeth begins wondering if he will one day be king.

When Macbeth meets Duncan again, the king announces to all that his son Malcolm will be his heir. Duncan also plans to honor Macbeth with a visit to his castle. Macbeth now thinks he might have to kill the king for the prophecy to come true. He writes to his wife about it, and she begins plotting how the deed might be accomplished. When the king arrives, he is wined and dined. Behind closed doors, Macbeth balks at killing the king, who is also his kinsman and his guest. But Lady Macbeth accuses him of not being manly enough. He agrees to go through with their plot.

The Murder

Lady Macbeth drugs the king's guards, and Macbeth kills the king after everyone has gone to bed. They plan to place the blame on the guards. Early in the morning, some noblemen and the king's sons, Malcolm and Donalbain, come for the king. Nobleman Macduff finds the king dead. Macbeth kills the guards, supposedly because he is so angry at them for killing the king. Malcolm and Donalbain are not fooled, however, and agree to disappear—one to England and one to Ireland—before anyone tries to assassinate them as well. Macbeth is named king.

Because the witches have said Banquo's descendants will be kings, Macbeth now thinks he has to do away with Banquo as well. During the banquet to celebrate his coronation, Macbeth's hired assassins arrive to tell him privately they've killed Banquo but Banquo's son Fleance escaped. After they leave, Macbeth sees Banquo's ghost at the table. He is horrified and speaks to the ghost, but to the guests it appears he is talking to the air. Lady Macbeth sends the guests home. Traumatized, Macbeth wants to meet with the witches again to find out how he can ensure he will remain on the throne.

Keeping the Throne

The witches tell Macbeth no man born of a woman can kill him and he will not be overthrown until Birnam Wood, a forest, comes to Dunsinane Hill, where Macbeth's castle is located. Since all men are born from women and since forests cannot move, Macbeth is reassured. Macduff flees to England, where he meets with Malcolm to plan a war to overthrow Macbeth. After Macbeth finds out Macduff has left Scotland, he sends assassins to kill his family and heirs. When Macduff learns of the brutal murder of his family, he is even more determined to take down Macbeth.

Enter Macduff

Suffering pangs of conscience, Lady Macbeth has taken to sleepwalking—seemingly washing blood off her hands. Soon afterward, Macbeth receives news that Lady Macbeth has killed herself. Meanwhile, Macduff

Macbeth is terrified when he sees Banquo's ghost at the dining table.

and Malcolm invade Scotland and are joined by rebel forces at Birnam Wood. The soldiers cut down tree branches to march with and disguise their numbers; this makes it appear as if the forest were moving. Macbeth and Macduff meet on the battlefield. At first Macbeth doesn't want to kill Macduff because he has already done him so much harm. When Macduff says he was cut out of his mother's womb rather than born in the usual way, Macbeth engages with him and is killed. Malcolm becomes king, and order is restored to Scotland.

Fall of the Tragic Hero

*S*ometimes a character who falls from grace never achieves redemption. Such downfalls in Greek tragedies follow a classic pattern in which a protagonist is destroyed by a combination of personal weakness—a tragic flaw—and supernatural forces outside of their control. The Greek archetype of the tragic hero occurs in many stories. Examining the origin of the character's tragic flaw can add depth to the story.

Macbeth and *Things Fall Apart*, although written centuries apart, have common threads. Both works focus on a main character with a tragic flaw that leads to his final failure. Both main characters have ideas about masculinity that contribute to their tragic flaws. *Macbeth* and *Things Fall Apart* both use the Greek

Macbeth never achieves redemption.

archetype of a tragic hero to fashion protagonists who irrevocably fall from grace because of deeply ingrained flaws related to their ideas of masculinity.

When Macbeth is tempted with unlimited power, his ambition and ideas about what qualities make him manly are awakened, and he violates society's law and his own code of ethics to get what he wants. When Macbeth learns the Prince of Cumberland, the king's son Malcolm, has been named as successor, he must overcome his natural goodness to pursue the path of unbridled ambition. He says, "The Prince of Cumberland! That is a step / On which I must fall down or else o'erleap / For in my way it lies. Stars, hide your fires; / Let not light see my black and deep desires."[1] Macbeth's tragic flaw

Once he is tempted with unlimited power, Macbeth will go to great lengths to obtain it, including murder.

of overwhelming ambition begins his fall from grace. Then, when Macbeth has second thoughts, his ideas about his own masculinity keep him from turning back. Later, he tells Lady Macbeth that he has changed his mind about killing the king and is trying to do the right thing. But his wife knows his weakness and answers, "Art thou afeard / To be the same in thine own act and valor / As thou art in desire?"[2] Lady Macbeth accuses her husband of lacking manliness by not sticking to his plan. Since it is important for Macbeth to view himself as masculine and powerful, he agrees to continue down his dark path.

Argument Two

In the second argument, the author continues her examination of Macbeth's fall from grace. The second argument is: "Macbeth fights to hold on to his illegal power to sustain his ambition and because submitting to defeat would be unmanly."

Macbeth fights to hold on to his illegal power to sustain his ambition and because submitting to defeat would be unmanly. First Macbeth has assassins murder Banquo. And although Macbeth is fearful when he sees Banquo's ghost, he is not sorry for what he has done. Immediately after, he decides to go back to the witches to find out whether he can hold on to his crown. He tells his wife, "For my own good, / All causes shall give way. I am in blood / Stepped in so far, that, should I wade no more, / Returning were as tedious as go o'er," meaning he has come so far in his evil he cannot turn back.[3] When he meets the witches again, they tell him to beware of Macduff. As soon as Macbeth hears that Macduff has fled to England, he gives the order to wipe out his entire family. Even after hearing his beloved wife has killed herself, he seems more focused on his ambition than on grief for his wife. He fights bravely to the end to hold on to his ill-gotten gains, but he has no regrets. He tells Macduff at their final meeting that

When Macbeth and Macduff battle for the throne, failure is not an option for Macbeth.

he would rather die than be ruled by Malcolm, saying, "Lay on, Macduff, / And damned be him that first cries 'Hold, Enough!'"[4] To Macbeth, submitting to the rule of another man would be emasculating.

Okonkwo in *Things Fall Apart* also fits the classical

model of a tragic hero who is undone by a fatal flaw—a rigidity of character based on a deeply rooted fear of being considered weak or unmanly. Okonkwo shows his manliness in violent and destructive ways to prove he is not like his weak father. For example, he beats one of his wives during the Week of Peace because she has failed to make his afternoon meal. Exhibiting any sort of violence during this time is an offense against the earth goddess, so Okonkwo is heavily fined. His worst offense, however, is killing his foster son, Ikemefuna, a hostage who has come to live with him. When the Oracle declares the boy must die, none of the men expect Okonkwo to take part in the ritual killing. Yet even though he loves the boy, he insists on taking part and winds up dealing the death blow. Finally, Okonkwo shoots off his gun as part of a funeral ritual and accidentally kills the son of the man who is being buried. He knew the gun did not work properly, but he took the risk anyway.

When Okonkwo returns from exile, his old world is

Argument Four

The final argument is: "When Okonkwo returns from exile, his old world is gone, but he chooses to die rather than face the prospect of living in a society where a new culture is changing what it means to be a man."

gone, but he chooses to die rather than face the prospect of living in a society where a new culture is changing what it means to be a man. The white colonialists have arrived in Umuofia during his exile, bringing a government and a new religion. Some of the people are converting, which drives a wedge between the old and new orders. Okonkwo's eldest son, Nwoye, who has been treated brutally by his father because he is softer and "weaker," converts to Christianity because he is attracted to its message of acceptance. Yet, it is impossible for Okonkwo to see his role in his son's conversion. After several conflicts with the newcomers, Okonkwo urges other villagers to go to war with the white man. Okonkwo continues to act out his aggressive tragic flaw when he kills one of the white messengers. At that point, rather than be arrested and face the white man's justice, Okonkwo takes his own life. Because of his rigid adherence to his idea of masculinity, Okonkwo leaves himself with no choice but a dishonorable death and an outcast's burial.

In both of these works, the protagonists—through their own actions and events beyond their control—suffer a quick fall from grace, into an abyss with no exit. Both have heroic qualities but also a deep character

Macbeth's blind ambition and focus on his own masculinity lead to his downfall.

Conclusion

The conclusion restates the thesis and summarizes the arguments made in support of the thesis. The author asserts that both characters' ideas about masculinity lead to their fall from grace.

flaw. Their focus on their ideas of what it means to be masculine leads to their downfall. These fatal flaws have disastrous consequences for both men, who end up unredeemed.

Thinking Critically

Now it's your turn to assess the essay. Consider these questions:

1. Do you think the works' authors would agree with the writer's assessment of these characters as tragic heroes? Why or why not?

2. Is it reasonable to think Macbeth or Okonkwo could have redeemed themselves in the context of their cultures?

3. Do you feel sympathy for Macbeth and Okonkwo? Why or why not?

Other Approaches

This essay is just one possible approach to thinking about how the theme of a fall from grace can be considered in *Macbeth* and *Things Fall Apart*. Here are two additional ways to think about the same theme. One considers Okonkwo's fall from grace as a heroic tale. The other focuses on how temptation leads to Macbeth's fall from grace.

Okonkwo's Suicide as a Triumph over Oppressors

In *Thing Fall Apart*, Okonkwo's community is struggling with an influx of white missionaries who are changing their way of life. Another approach to *Things Fall Apart* could look at Okonkwo's fall from grace as a heroic tale of a brave man's last stand against an oppressive conqueror. A thesis statement that takes this approach could be: Okonkwo's unjust fall from grace proves he is a hero who upholds the values of his culture and triumphs over the conquerors by not allowing them to punish him.

Temptation and Fall from Grace

In *Macbeth*, the witches prophesize Macbeth will become king. Before this, Macbeth doesn't have this ambition. Another approach to an essay on *Macbeth* might be to emphasize the role of the prophecy as the temptation that triggers Macbeth's fall from grace. A thesis statement for an essay that takes this approach could be: The three witches tempt Macbeth with the idea of becoming king, which leads Macbeth to his downfall.

Analyze It!

Now that you have examined the theme of a fall from grace, are you ready to perform your own analysis? You have read that this type of evaluation can help you look at literature in a new way and make you pay attention to certain issues you may not have otherwise recognized. So, why not look for a fall from grace theme in one or more of your favorite books?

First, choose the work you want to analyze. What is the main fall from grace? Do characters grow or change as a result of their falls from grace? Are they able to achieve redemption? If you choose to compare the theme in more than one work, what do they have in common? How do they differ? Next, write a specific question about the theme that interests you. Then you can form your thesis, which should provide the answer to that question. Your thesis is the most important part of your analysis and offers an argument about the work, considering the theme, its effect on the characters, or what it says about society or the world. Recall that the thesis statement typically appears at the very end of the introductory paragraph of your essay. It is usually only one sentence long.

After you have written your thesis, find evidence to back it up. Good places to start are in the work itself or in journals or articles that discuss what other people have said about it. You may also want to read about the author or creator's life so you can get a sense of what factors may have affected the creative process. This can be especially useful if you are considering how the theme connects to history or the author's intent.

You should also explore parts of the book that seem to disprove your thesis and create an argument against them. As you do this, you might want to address what others have written about the book. Their quotes may help support your claim.

Before you start analyzing a work, think about the different arguments made in this book. Reflect on how evidence supporting the thesis was presented. Did you find that some of the techniques used to back up the arguments were more convincing than others? Try these methods as you prove your thesis in your own critique.

When you are finished writing your critique, read it over carefully. Is your thesis statement understandable? Do the supporting arguments flow logically, with the topic of each paragraph clearly stated? Can you add any information that would present your readers with a stronger argument in favor of your thesis? Were you able to use quotes from the book, as well as from other critics, to enhance your ideas? Did you see the work in a new light?

Glossary

adultery
Sex between a married person and someone who is not that person's wife or husband.

atone
To make up for doing something bad by doing something good.

characterize
To portray and describe a character in a work.

comatose
Unable to function.

communism
A system of government in which all property is publically owned.

emasculate
To make unmanly.

lechery
Offensive lustfulness.

magistrate
A judge in a lower court.

morality
Beliefs about what is right behavior and what is wrong behavior.

motivation
The reason behind doing something.

pledge
A document promising payment of a debt.

protagonist
The main character in a book, movie, play, poem, or other work.

sledge
A large sleigh or vehicle mounted on runners that people can sit in.

thane
A Scottish nobleman who owns land and is obligated to perform service to his king.

traffic
A flow of communication.

Characteristics
AND CLASSICS

Fall from grace is a common theme in literature. Many fall from grace stories also include the theme of redemption.

This theme often includes:

- A character who falls away from the righteous or moral path
- A character who is at odds with society's idea of morality
- Supporting characters that may attempt to save the character who has fallen from grace or lead the character deeper into evil
- An attempt at redemption which can be either successful or unsuccessful
- A fatal flaw in a character that prevents his or her redemption
- A selfless act that earns the character redemption

Some famous works with a fall from grace are:

- The ancient Greek myth of Prometheus
- Shakespeare's *King Lear*
- Milton's *Paradise Lost*
- Victor Hugo's *Les Misérables*
- Edith Wharton's *Ethan Frome*
- Flannery O'Connor's "A Good Man Is Hard to Find"
- Anakin Skywalker in the Star Wars films

References

Achebe, Chinua. "The Novelist as Teacher." *Morning Yet on Creation Day*. Garden City, NY: Anchor, 1975. Print.

Achebe, Chinua. *Things Fall Apart*. New York: Ballantine, 1959. Print.

Dostoevsky, Fyodor. *Crime and Punishment*. Trans. Richard Pevear and Larissa Volokhonsky. New York: Vintage, 1993. Print.

Gascoigne, Bamber. "History of Nigeria." HistoryWorld, 2001. Web. 15 Jan. 2015.

"Hollywood Blacklist." *United States History*. Online Highways, n.d. Web. 15 Jan. 2015.

"Macbeth: Background." *Bitesize*. BBC, 2014. Web. 15 Jan. 2015.

Miller, Arthur. *The Crucible*. New York: Penguin, 1976. Print. 141.

"Salem Witch Trials." *History Topics*. A&E Television Networks, 2015. Web. 15 Jan. 2015.

Shakespeare, William. *Macbeth*. New York: Modern Library, 2009. Print.

Shelley, Mary. *Frankenstein or The Modern Prometheus*. Mineola, NY: Dover, 1994. Print.

Additional
RESOURCES

Further Readings

Bloom, Harold, ed. *Mary Shelley*. New York: Bloom's Literary
    Criticism, 2008. Print.

Hawker, Louise, ed. *Colonialism In Chinua Achebe's "Things Fall Apart."*
    Farmington Hills, MI: Greenhaven, 2010. Print.

Johnson, Claudia Durst. *Justice in Arthur Miller's "The Crucible."*
    Detroit: Greenhaven, 2009. Print

Kesselring, Mari. *How to Analyze the Works of William Shakespeare.*
    Minneapolis: Abdo, 2013. Print.

Websites

To learn more about Essential Literary Themes, visit
booklinks.abdopublishing.com. These links are routinely
monitored and updated to provide the most current information
available.

Places to Visit

The Bakken Museum
Frankenstein's Laboratory
3537 Zenith Avenue South
Minneapolis, MN 55416
612-926-3878
http://www.thebakken.org
With a focus on the history of electricity, this museum stages a scene from *Frankenstein* and provides information about author Mary Shelley.

Salem Witch Museum
19 ½ North Washington Square
Salem, MA 01970
978-744-1692
http://www.salemwitchmuseum.com
This museum provides information about the real Salem witch trials of 1692 as well as tours of historic sites related to the event.

Shakespeare's Globe Theatre
21 New Globe Walk
Bankside
London SE1 9DT
England
+44-(0)20-7902-1400
http://www.shakespearesglobe.com
Modeled after the original Globe Theatre where some of Shakespeare's plays were first performed, the Globe explores Shakespeare's work and hosts performances.

Source Notes

Chapter 1. Introduction to Themes in Literature
None.

Chapter 2. An Overview of *The Crucible*
1. Arthur Miller. *The Crucible.* New York: Penguin, 1976. Print. 9.
2. Ibid. 58.
3. Ibid. 126.

Chapter 3. Moral Compass in *The Crucible*
1. Arthur Miller. *The Crucible.* New York: Penguin, 1976. Print. 27.
2. Ibid. 19.
3. Ibid. 35.
4. Ibid. 102.
5. Ibid. 126.
6. Ibid. 131.
7. Ibid. 141.
8. Ibid.

Chapter 4. An Overview of *Crime and Punishment*
None.

Chapter 5. Biblical Fall in *Crime and Punishment*
1. Fyodor Dostoevsky. *Crime and Punishment.* Trans. Richard Pevear and Larissa Volokhonsky. New York: Vintage, 1993. Print. 65.
2. Ibid. 23.
3. Ibid. 326.
4. Ibid. 420.
5. Ibid. 549.

Chapter 6. An Overview of *Frankenstein*

1. Mary Shelley. *Frankenstein or The Modern Prometheus*. Mineola, NY: Dover, 1994. Print. 11.
2. Ibid. 68.
3. Ibid. 121.

Chapter 7. A Cautionary Tale

1. Mary Shelley. *Frankenstein or The Modern Prometheus*. Mineola, NY: Dover, 1994. Print. 12.
2. Ibid. 57.
3. Ibid. 142.

Chapter 8. Overviews of *Thing Fall Apart* and *Macbeth*

None.

Chapter 9. Fall of the Tragic Hero

1. William Shakespeare. *Macbeth*. New York: Modern Library, 2009. Print. 33–34.
2. Ibid. 39.
3. Ibid. 66–67.
4. Ibid. 98.

Index

About the Author

Maryellen Lo Bosco is a writer, editor, and educator. She has worked for many publishing organizations. As a teacher, she has worked for the New York City Department of Education, teaching in Queens, New York. She has been a writing instructor at Suffolk Community College (SCC) and Hofstra University in New York and currently tutors students in SCC's Writing Studio. She has a master's in English and comparative literature from Columbia University and a bachelor's in English and writing from Queens College, City University of New York.